FUND RAISING REALITIES
EVERY BOARD MEMBER
MUST FACE

A 1-Hour Crash Course
on Raising Major Gifts
for Nonprofit Organizations

FUND RAISING REALITIES EVERY BOARD MEMBER MUST FACE

A 1-Hour Crash Course
on Raising Major Gifts
for Nonprofit Organizations

David Lansdowne

Emerson
& Church
PUBLISHERS

Printed in the United States of America

Library of Congress Catalog
Card Number: 96-84332

ISBN 1-889102-10-5

17 16 15 14 13 12 11

This text is printed on acid-free paper.

Copies of this book are available from the
publisher at discount when purchased in
quantity for boards of directors or staff.

Emerson & Church, Publishers
P.O. Box 338
Medfield, MA 02052
Tel. 508-359-0019
www.emersonandchurch.com

To Miss October

An extraordinary reality

The Best Pairing Since Venus & Serena ...

FUND RAISING REALITIES and
Jerold Panas' Classic Book, ASKING

It ranks right up there with public speaking. Nearly all of us fear it. And yet it's critical to our success. *Asking for money*. It makes even the stout-hearted quiver.

But now comes a book, *Asking: A 59-Minute Guide to Everything Board Members, Staff and Volunteers Must Know to Secure the Gift*. And short of a medical elixir, it's the next best thing for emboldening you, your board members and volunteers to ask with skill, finesse ... and powerful results.

Jerold Panas, who as a staff person, board member and volunteer has secured gifts ranging from $50 to $50 million, understands the art of asking perhaps better than anyone in America.

He has harnessed all of his knowledge and experience and produced a landmark book.

What *Asking* convincingly shows – and one reason staff will applaud the book and board members will devour it – is that it doesn't take stellar communication skills to be an effective asker.

Nearly everyone, regardless of their persuasive ability, can become an effective fundraiser if they follow Jerold Panas' step-by-step guidelines.

Jerold Panas • 108 pp. • $24.95
Emerson & Church, Publishers
ISBN 1889102172 • *Quantity Discounts Available*

PREFACE

This book could easily have been titled: *Everything a Board Member Needs to Know About Fund Raising and Not One Sentence More.*

That's because it was written to give board members a command of only the essentials -- a solid grasp of what works in fund raising, why it works, and how to use this accepted wisdom to your best advantage.

To be successful at raising money, board members don't require a detailed understanding of methodology. And thankfully so, because most have neither the time nor in all likelihood the inclination to explore the subject in depth. That is the role of staff.

What those who serve on nonprofit boards need is a working knowledge of techniques that have proven successful over time. It is my hope this book provides that, and nothing more.

CONTENTS

THE
REALITIES

1

THE MISSION MUST BE DEFINED

————◆————

Before beginning a fund raising drive, board members and staff alike must be clear about the goals of the organization.

Too often, those involved assume there is general agreement. But more commonly trustees have an indistinct sense of the organization's purpose and its aims for the future.

When preparing for a campaign, not only must you revisit your goals, but the board must also endorse them wholeheartedly.

One way to reach a healthy consensus is to conduct a half-day or full-day retreat, during which board members, along with staff, explore a wide range of fundamental questions:

❑ Why does your organization exist in the first place?

❑ What makes your organization better, or more effective, than similar ones in the community?

❑ Are your priorities clear?

❑ What are your major strengths and weaknesses?

❑ How can you improve your services?

❑ What are your long- and short-range objectives? And,

❑ Where do your resources come from and are they sufficient?

It's essential that your organization's key leaders and volunteers participate in this process. In fact, a self-analysis of this kind is a superb way to involve people who will be important to your future.

It gives influential prospects a voice in determining your organization's direction and motivates them to work harder and contribute more. They will, after all, want to realize plans they themselves have helped to shape.

Before committing large sums of money, you can be sure your major prospects will ask probing questions. If you expect to secure their support, you must be able to articulate your mission and describe realistic plans for reaching your goals.

2

THE BUCK STOPS HERE

—◆—

If there is a first principle in fund raising, it is this: the board of directors has the responsibility for ensuring that the organization's mission is carried out, and of necessity this means finding the resources to do so.

The logic is irrefutable: board members own the organization and are its stewards. If they, who purportedly are the strongest advocates, won't take a lead role in raising money, why should anyone else?

To demonstrate their commitment, board members must first make a generous gift proportionate to their means, and second, agree to devote adequate time and energy to assure success.

This kind of support sends an unmistakable message to prospective donors, namely, that the organization means business.

If members of the board are reluctant to take responsibility, it is probably because 1) they don't understand the importance of assuming the helm in fund raising, and 2) they're afraid they will be required to ask others for money.

In truth, board members *will* often be required to ask, but in a well-run fund raising program they can participate in other ways too. Some can solicit, others can plan special events, still others can help with researching prospects, or making introductions for others.

Almost always, organizations that raise substantial money have knowledgeable and active trustees. By the same token, causes which scrape by usually have indifferent board members who are unwilling to accept their role.

Lacking a fully-committed board, it will not be difficult to involve others, it will be practically impossible.

3

EVERYONE DISLIKES ASKING

◆

Rare is the trustee who enjoys fund raising.

If you think it's significantly easier for others to ask for money, you are mistaken. Everyone has the same doubts, fears, and anxieties as you. If it appears easier for others, it is probably because they've faced up to the fact that fund raising is essential to the survival of the organization.

Undoubtedly, you'll recognize some of the excuses below:

❑ I give my time, that's enough.

❑ I don't know the right people.

❑ Fund raising is belittling.

❑ Raising money is the role of the development staff.

❑ My work on the board has to do with policy.

Strive to put these and all other excuses aside. Recognize that board members have two basic responsibilities: one is to set policy, the other is to ensure resources. Both are critical, and neither can be skirted.

If the job of raising money is to get done, each trustee must get on with the assignment, and overcome the natural tendency to procrastinate.

A campaign with firm deadlines, tight schedules, reporting sessions, and follow-up phone calls will help, as will workshops, half-day briefings, and accompanying an experienced solicitor on a call.

Perhaps the best salve for anxiety, however, is to keep in mind that you aren't asking for yourself, nor do you have anything to gain financially, nor are you seeking something from others which you yourself have not given.

Your position is unassailable: you are a volunteer working on behalf of a cause that's in the public interest and serves the general good.

4

BE READY
OR REGROUP

The error most commonly made in fund raising — especially major gifts fund raising — is deciding to make a push before you're ready.

Serious campaigns demand a great deal of time, effort, and resources, and before you jump in, it's critical to determine your organization's readiness.

To do this, you must answer some very fundamental questions:

❑ Are your organization's goals unmistakably clear?

❑ Are you seen as a worthwhile asset to your community?

❑ Do board members believe the cause is important?

❑ Will they contribute time *and* money?

❏ Can you make a persuasive case for funding your project?

❏ Do you have the required leadership for the campaign, including a candidate for general chairperson?

In addition to these basic questions — which must be answered in the affirmative — there's the all-important last question: Do you have enough legitimate prospects?

To be successful, you'll normally need about three times the number of potential donors for every one gift you expect to receive. In other words, it usually take three "asks" to realize one gift.

When you review your prospect pool, ask yourself:

❏ How close are these people to our organization, and,

❏ How ready are they to be solicited?

And don't kid yourself. Prospects only have real and immediate potential if they've been cultivated and are familiar, if not deeply involved, with your work.

You can't raise money, at least big money, casually. Unless the board commits to the campaign, with able leadership and generous giving, you're best advised to retreat and reexamine.

5

MONEY COSTS MONEY

◆

A fund raising campaign can be an expensive proposition, especially up front. There are any number of outlays, including professional counsel, printing, office space, and clerical help to name just a few. Unless you have adequate start-up money, think seriously about delaying your campaign.

Of course you can attempt a hand-to-mouth effort. That is, try to raise money and then pay your expenses from these funds. But almost always this approach fails. In addition, you won't attract good leadership nor will you inspire much confidence in your prospective donors.

How much, specifically, should it cost you to raise money?

There are no simple answers. Some established

organizations spend less than 10 percent of their campaign goal, while many new groups — and more than a few inefficient ones — spend 50 cents or more for every dollar raised.

It depends on your variables:

❑ The methods of fund raising you're using (personal solicitation, direct mail, special events, planned giving, grantseeking).

❑ The amount you're attempting to raise.

❑ The number of prospects you have.

❑ Your plans for cultivating potential donors.

❑ Whether you'll be hiring professional counsel.

❑ Where your prospects live.

❑ The length of your drive. And,

❑ Your current level of support.

The cost of fund raising is a complicated issue. Spending lavishly won't guarantee success; often it can backfire. But having little or nothing to spend is almost a certain forecaster of failure.

6

THE RATIONALE MUST BE SOUND

---◆---

What is your organization's purpose? How easily can you state it? Why are you seeking funds? For what specific needs? Why should people give to you rather than to another group?

Before setting out to raise money, each organization must think through the *rationale* for its appeal and put it in writing.

Simply because your cause is worthy and needs funding — as do thousands of others — won't rouse anyone, no matter how well organized your effort. You must have a clear case.

The document in which you lay out your arguments is your "case statement." In essence it is your organization's sales pitch.

It tells donors and prospects who you are, what you're trying to accomplish, and why. It describes your history, purpose, and plans. But, most importantly, it outlines the reasons a person should invest in your organization and the benefits that will result.

Your case statement needn't be long or elaborate. More important is that it be tastefully prepared, well-written, simple, and free of exaggeration.

If yours is a simple appeal for funds, a two-page letter might suffice. On the other hand, you might need an eight to ten page brochure for a multi-million dollar drive.

What matters more than length and looks is that your case be written from the perspective of your prospects, clearly showing that by helping your organization they will be helping themselves and the communities in which they live and work.

Presenting your organization in its most favorable light, a case statement is not a direct request for funds. It is, instead, a persuasive support piece that reinforces the actual request and communicates that the donor's gift will indeed make a difference.

7

INDIVIDUALS
ARE THE TARGET

◆

Of the billions contributed to charitable organizations each year, roughly 85 percent comes from individuals (90 percent if you include bequests). This percentage, with slight fluctuations, has stayed the same for decades.

Thus, while major grants from foundations and corporations usually make the news, individuals account for the real action.

It's only logical, then, to concentrate most of your fund raising efforts on this promising source and not on corporations and foundations.

Despite the soundness of this strategy, many people still focus a disproportionate amount of their time on corporations and foundations — most likely because they fear rejection.

While foundations and corporations are by no

means easy targets, they do *expect* to be solicited. And, since they prefer a proposal or letter, the hardest part of fund raising — standing in front of a prospect and actually asking — is eliminated.

By all means, pursue corporations and foundations, but don't spend a large share of your time doing so. Keep your priorities straight by remembering these three things:

❑ Most private support comes from individuals.

❑ Much of our nation's wealth is in the form of real property, owned by individuals. And,

❑ Individuals need not adhere to particular priorities; they can give to whatever they wish, whenever they wish.

One final note: you might think that, with so many organizations asking, the donor pool is shrinking. Not so. Studies show that two out of five people feel they don't give enough, confirming the enormity of the potential.

8

THE BUCK STARTS HERE

◆

To be most effective, fund raising must proceed from the "inside out."

This means solicitation begins with the organization's "family," its board, staff, and other key volunteers, and only then reaches out to others.

For this reason, board members must realize that until they themselves give, and give generously, few others will be inclined to do so. And the key word here is "generously."

Potential donors, including corporations and foundations, want to know what the board has contributed. And if these gifts have been token, then prospective donors will rightfully follow suit with small amounts.

Their reasoning is sound. Why should they

give generously if those closest to the organization — the trustees — don't feel it's important enough to do so?

For a campaign to succeed, it's often necessary for the board to contribute upwards of 20 percent of the total goal. If members can't do this, then the campaign is usually in trouble from the start.

There will be some who insist they give their time and this should be sufficient. But while time and money are both essential, one without the other isn't enough. A volunteer gives time; a donor gives money. But a board member has the responsibility to give both.

Then, too, some will say they can't afford to give the amounts required, in which case the goal may be too large, at least until you identify enough legitimate prospects.

Finally, there will be some board members who have the capacity to give but don't yet appreciate the goals enough to make a significant commitment. In this case, the board itself hasn't been educated fully about the goal and the organization isn't ready for a campaign.

If it is next to impossible to raise a substantial portion of your goal from the board, take this as a warning that your entire campaign needs reassessing.

9

A FEW CONTRIBUTE THE MOST

◆

More than a half century of fund raising, and the experience garnered from thousands of campaigns, has shown that one pattern continually recurs: in nearly every campaign a very small number of donors contribute most of the money.

Those in the field call this the *90/10* rule: 90 percent of the funds you receive come from about 10 percent of your prospects.

The reasons are fairly simple. To begin with, wealth isn't distributed equally in society, so most people simply can't afford to make large gifts. Too, even when assets are available, not everyone feels the need to give. Finally, no matter how much they might like to, many people just can't give any contribution.

What this means is that to reach your goal you must devote most of your time and effort — as much as 90 percent — to your top prospects and rely on sizable gifts from them.

Big givers are, in fact, so important you should approach each of them as a campaign in itself — taking care to find the right solicitor, equip him or her with your most persuasive arguments, and then thoroughly train the asker.

It is just this kind of painstaking preparation that usually makes the difference in reaching your goal.

Whatever the scope of your campaign, and regardless of whether you consider a major gift to be $100 or $100,000, your campaign will falter without major donors and a handful of stretch gifts from your 10 most promising prospects.

10

GIFTS NEED PLOTTING

◆

It is foolish to embark upon a fund raising drive until you have a good idea of the number and size of gifts needed to reach your goal. A gift table, which is a geometric progression based on accumulated fund raising experience, provides this information.

Most often gift tables are used in capital campaigns, but the method works equally well for annual giving programs.

Assume your goal is $1 million. Drawing upon the "Rule of Thirds" described on page 35, the top ten gifts you seek should total approximately $350,000 or roughly one-third of your goal, with one gift bringing in 10 percent.

The next 100 gifts should produce about the same amount -- $350,000.

And the remainder of your gifts should bring in $300,000 or the final 30 percent.

A gift table is sobering, and rightly so. It says, in effect, that without gifts of the sizes indicated, the entire effort has little if any chance of success.

Among the many purposes a gift table serves are the following:

❑ It outlines the number and size of gifts you need to reach your goal.

❑ It serves as a kind of reality check for your board and major prospects.

❑ It is used during your feasibility study to determine the validity of your projected goal.

❑ It can raise the sights of prospective donors.

❑ It's an excellent indicator of your progress to date. And,

❑ It's a valuable evaluation tool once your campaign is over.

Understand that a gift table isn't a precise instrument, however. There are simply too many variables to cast in stone an accurate table for every campaign.

11

THINK IN THIRDS

◆

The rule of thirds, borne out in campaign after campaign, states that one-third of your funds will come from your top 10 to 15 donors, with one gift equaling 10 percent of your goal.

One-third will come from your next 100 to 125 donors.

And the remaining one-third will come from all others.

For a $1 million campaign, the rule of thirds plotted on a gift table might look like this:

Gift Amount	# of Gifts	Total
$100,000	1	$100,000
50,000	2	$100,000
25,000	4	$100,000
10,000	20	$200,000
2,000	150	$300,000
Under 1,000	many	$200,000

While the percentages will sometimes fluctuate — for example, multi-million dollar campaigns will need perhaps 40 to 50 percent of the total from the top donors — the rule of thirds has stood the test of time.

You can, with a great degree of confidence, develop your table of gifts with this principle in mind. It will help you determine if in fact you have the necessary 10 to 15 top donors to ensure the success of your campaign.

12

INTERVIEWS
ARE REVEALING

◆

It is unwise to attempt a serious fund raising drive without first assessing your chances of success.

By interviewing prominent board members, major gift prospects, other potential donors, business leaders, and influential community leaders, you can learn a great deal about your fund raising potential and how people view your organization and proposed campaign.

A good *feasibility study*, as this process is called, typically includes 40 to 50 in-depth interviews, more if your goal is very large. And while it won't tell exactly what you can raise, a carefully done study will:

❏ Uncover your organization's strengths and weaknesses.

❏ Help you set a campaign goal.

❏ Bring important people closer to your project.

❏ Help identify leaders and prospects for your campaign. And,

❏ Tell you what your community thinks of your organization or project.

Once the interviews are completed, a final report usually recommends a dollar goal or goal range, identifies potential campaign leaders, and suggests a timetable and budget.

Sometimes a study will suggest delaying the campaign until certain corrective measures can be taken. Most often, these involve strengthening the board, improving the public's perception of the organization, and identifying and cultivating more prospects.

To assure objectivity, feasibility studies are often conducted by outside consultants.

13

CONSULTANTS WILL AND WON'T

———◆———

Conducting a major gifts campaign is a big job. Often too big for the staff alone, given their other responsibilities. Enter the fund raising consultant.

Just what is the role of this professional?

Well, let's first clarify what it is *not*.

❏ It is *not* to solicit money for you. That's the role of the board and, in some cases, the staff.

❏ It is *not* to wheel in hundreds of new prospects. The best ones you already know.

❏ It's *not* to replace the work of staff or board members. It is to supplement their work and enhance their knowledge.

In sum, the role of a consultant is *not* to raise money for you, it is to help *you* raise it.

In this regard, what the seasoned consultant *will* do is:

❑ Help you evaluate your needs.

❑ Uncover your strengths and weaknesses.

❑ Assess your fund raising potential.

❑ Outline a plan of action (if you're ready).

❑ Help prepare materials.

❑ Conduct trainings.

❑ Troubleshoot. And,

❑ Serve as a catalyst to keep your campaign moving.

An ideal consultant offers experience, objectivity, and independence. These qualities allow him or her to level with volunteer leaders and, when the occasion demands, voice concerns they may not care to hear.

14

NO GOAL, NO OBJECTIVE

———◆———

"Heck, we'll just raise all we can. We don't need a goal."

Those new to fund raising, or those unfamiliar with proven techniques, sometimes propose this. But unless it's your first time raising money, this approach is a mistake.

Every drive for funds needs a dollar goal. Your prospects won't take you seriously without one, or, just as bad, they'll assume you haven't thought out what you need.

When setting a goal, you must strike that delicate balance between what is feasible and what is challenging. On the one hand, your prospects must feel your goal is attainable or they may give only token sums. On the other hand, they must be sufficiently challenged by the goal to make a stretch gift.

For an annual drive, if your organization has raised yearly funds before, goal setting is relatively simple. Your goal will be based upon the results of the last three years.

Setting a capital campaign goal is more involved, however, and it depends on a number of important variables: your need for funds; the persuasiveness of your case; the financial capacity of your prospect list; your constituency's appreciation of your achievements; and the leadership of your campaign.

Some will argue for a high goal, believing it encourages campaigners to stretch.

Others insist on a low, achievable goal that leaves everyone filled with pride.

Still others lobby for a goal reflecting the exact costs of the project.

While each side has persuasive points, what is really needed in terms of a goal is careful thought to arrive at that certain number that inspires your volunteers, makes them work harder than they ever anticipated, and fills them with excitement when victory is achieved.

15

LIGHTEN THE LOAD

◆

Board members and staff cannot carry the total burden of a major gifts campaign, even a limited one. Volunteers are needed.

And while volunteers can be used for a variety of internal jobs such as reviewing lists, preparing mailings, and collecting data, their most important role is in soliciting gifts.

Why? Because of the many ways to raise money, the most effective — the most productive in terms of the *size* of gifts — is the personal, eyeball-to-eyeball approach. And to be able to see most of your prospects in person, ample numbers of volunteers will be needed.

Often you'll be able to attract them if you keep in mind the reasons why people volunteer: because *you ask them*; because they believe in your mission; because they want to improve their community; because they desire recognition; because they're susceptible to peer pressure; because they need visibility; or because it's helpful to their business.

To earn the full commitment of volunteers, you must invite them to participate not just in the soliciting phase of your campaign but in the preparation as well — in goal setting, developing your case, rating the gift potential of prospects, and planning cultivation activities.

Throughout this whole process, keep in mind that people work best if:

❑ Each has a single task, clearly defined, such as calling upon one prospect per week.

❑ You don't require attendance at too many formal meetings.

❑ The service is relatively quick and limited to a short time period.

❑ The person is publicly recognized for his or her contribution.

Volunteers are instrumental to a campaign. But without skillful management you'll end up serving them rather than vice versa.

16

THOSE WHO SET THE GOAL, SET THEIR SIGHTS

◆

To a large extent it is the role of the CEO to identify the resources your organization needs. This list of budgetary items then serves as a backdrop against which your goal setting process begins.

But once the background work is done, there's no better way for fund raising leadership to begin motivating top campaign workers than to involve them actively in setting the campaign's dollar goal.

When volunteers have a say in the process, when they can voice their opinions and take part in the debate, they'll feel they "own" the campaign and be manifestly more committed to making it a success.

Not that volunteers can do it alone. Setting a goal, even for seasoned pros, isn't easy. Factors such as your organization's history, your prospect pool, the urgency of your appeal, the findings of your feasibility study — all of these will influence your final figure. And, without staff or professional guidance, volunteers will often set goals that are too low or simply unattainable.

But they should participate, as they are the pivotal players who will determine the success of your campaign. As such they won't appreciate being brought in as soldiers after the most important decisions have been made.

The judgment of these volunteers is then reviewed by the campaign management team, which in turn passes it before the board of directors for review.

Using volunteers to help you set your goal is more time-consuming than doing it by executive fiat. But to exclude campaign workers from the process is to lose a golden opportunity to involve them deeply in your campaign.

17

PUBLICITY IS
NO SUBSTITUTE

◆

Don't expect publicity to raise money. It doesn't, at least most of the time.

The reasons are simple. To raise substantial money you must ask people in person, regardless of any well-placed stories. Secondly, most campaigns depend on a relatively small number of major donors — about 10 percent of the prospects — whose decision to give won't be much influenced by the media.

In fact, since it can be effective to solicit top prospects *before* your campaign goes public — in effect treating these special few as insiders — publicity in the early stages can actually work against you.

If it has a role in your campaign, publicity is simply to announce the drive, explain its purpose, and provide progress reports from time to time.

Those who rely on press releases and feature stories to raise funds tend either to be novices or people who aren't committed in the first place. They hope the media can do their work for them, and when this doesn't happen, they blame the failure not on themselves but on the lack of exposure.

Consider a publicity drive only if one of the following applies:

❑ If you're using an event to raise money and need to sell a great number of tickets.

❑ If your project benefits the general public, such as the refurbishing of a community park.

❑ If you're in a small town.

❑ If you're persuaded that publicity will stimulate your leadership to work harder.

❑ If you have a number of big donors who would like the attention.

❑ If you have a poor image.

❑ If you've already raised most of your goal and want to stimulate your campaign workers to complete their calls.

But even when any of these scenarios applies, remember that publicity is always an adjunct measure; the real action involves people asking people in person.

18

SPECIAL EVENTS CAN BE DOUBLE-EDGED

◆

When volunteers convene and the subject of raising money arises, often someone will suggest holding a dinner dance, gala, road race, or similar event. It usually sounds like a good idea, especially since selling tickets is a lot less threatening than eyeballing someone for a contribution.

But just as it's easy to get excited over a fashionable ball, it's easy as well to overlook the total costs associated with a special event. Before long, these expenses can exceed 50 percent of the revenue (as compared with 5 to 20 percent for major gifts campaigns).

Even when you're diligent and get a good number of products and services donated, still you'll need to pay for things such as a banquet hall, greens fees, and catering. Factor in printing, flowers, decorations, music, perhaps even travel and lodging, and the costs can become prohibitive.

Consuming as they do an extensive amount of time and resources, special events cannot match the cost-effectiveness of a person-to-person campaign.

In fact, in terms of the relative effectiveness of various fund raising methods, Henry Rosso, founder of The Fund Raising School, ranks special events near the bottom, behind team soliciting, one-on-one soliciting, soliciting by personal letter with a follow-up telephone call, and a personal telephone call by a peer with a follow-up letter.

Granted, there are sound reasons for holding an event: calling attention to your organization, educating and inspiring your current leaders and donors, attracting some new, potential leaders, and uncovering hidden constituents.

But before you go the events route, make sure you've planned well, you've allowed adequate preparation time, you have a realistic budget, ample numbers of people to work, and the know-how to get your event enough publicity.

And, yes, make sure you keep one important principle in mind: that your income must exceed your expenses.

19

FOREGO
THE FANCY

It is appalling how much time and money is wasted each year on fund raising materials.

How typical it is for board members *and* staff to squander weeks, if not months, laboring over the exact phrasing of their brochures, and then spend thousands of dollars printing them.

And to what end? Very little, as prospects usually give fleeting attention to these pieces.

You'll save precious resources and be a lot more effective if you get your story across as simply and as personally as possible.

In fact, your verbal presentation is far more important than any printed matter. This, coupled with an individually-tailored proposal for your top prospects will be far more impressive than any generic materials.

Understand, tasteful brochures and reports can play a role. For prospects, they can create a favorable impression. For solicitors, they're often a crutch to lean on when nervousness sets in. And for board members who participate in developing them, campaign materials can build camaraderie and focus attention on the organization's goals and objectives.

But always recognize printed materials or videos for what they are — *supporting* documents and nothing more. The basic ones to consider include:

❏ A case statement, either typed or printed.

❏ A one-page outline of the case for the solicitor to use when talking with the prospect.

❏ A folder listing the various ways a prospect can give, covering the tax advantages and the mechanics of making outright and planned gifts of cash, securities, or property.

❏ A guide offering suggestions for soliciting prospects.

❏ A question and answer sheet, addressing the questions prospects are most likely to ask.

❏ A list of named gift opportunities.

❏ A pledge card or subscription form or letter of intent.

It bears repeating that a brochure doesn't raise money, the solicitor does. Never think a printed piece can take the place of sitting across from the prospect, looking him or her in the eye, and requesting a specific gift.

20

WEALTH ALONE DOESN'T DETERMINE

◆

Those new to fund raising often make a fatal assumption: that if an individual is well-to-do, stoking his desire to give will be relatively easy. After all, what's $10,000 or $20,000 to a multi-millionaire?

Wrong.

Regardless of their income, people aren't casual about parting with money.

They have the same thoughts as you. Who is asking and for how much? Why me? For what purpose? Why now, and how soon again? All of these questions run through their mind.

In addition, donors have giving habits. Based upon prior association and personal experience, they make regular gifts to their favorite organizations.

Consequently, even a wealthy person won't give much until you make your organization important to him or her. You have to earn the commitment, in other words.

And when you think about it, this only makes sense. Why would a relative stranger give you a major gift when there are other organizations to which he or she feels closer and more connected?

Most major donors follow a logical progression. First they become interested in an organization, then get more involved, then deepen their commitment further by making a large gift.

In sum, they are sophisticated people who won't give until they're ready.

21

THAT YOU NEED, WON'T INSPIRE

◆

Although you must clearly understand why you're seeking funds — and the end to which the money will be put — when you go out to visit prospects, you should focus on the *deeds* the money will accomplish, not on the needs of your organization.

Donors give, not because you have a need, but to meet worthy objectives. They want their money to help, to make something better, to fill a community need.

And while factors such as recognition, guilt, pressure, fear, and gratitude often come into play, people primarily give when they feel inspired — when they're confident a cause is worthy and is led by people with integrity .

That's why it's much easier — and more

pleasant as well — to raise money for a positive end than, say, a negative one like overcoming a deficit. It's hardly inspiring to any prospect to bail out a strapped organization. In fact, doubts about fiscal management are sure to send prospects scurrying.

Granted, there's nothing wrong with asking for help, especially when you're doing so on behalf of a good cause. But you must ask in a way that renders hope, that makes people proud to be associated with your effort. That's something far different than asking simply because your organization needs their money.

22

STRANGERS SELDOM GIVE

—— ◆ ——

Very rare is the person who gives generously before becoming familiar with a cause. In other words, don't depend on strangers to make extraordinary gifts.

To attract real support, you must involve your best prospects in your organization — a process known as *cultivation* — as soon as possible. Not only will they turn out to be your best contributors, they may well become your most impassioned solicitors.

Give these key people the opportunity to see your organization and its people up close. Invite them to serve on committees. Encourage them to attend meetings and strategy sessions. Seek their advice. Have them participate in your special events. In sum, do everything you can — with sincerity — to make your organization a significant part of their lives.

And do so regularly, not just when you need their financial backing. Like you they're smart enough to know when they're being wooed for their money alone.

The cultivation methods most commonly used are printed materials, organizational service (such as asking prospects to serve on committees), special events, and one-on-one attention.

It can be helpful, when developing a cultivation program, to group your top prospects into four categories: those whom you think are ready to give generously; those who will likely give with a bit more cultivation; those who require prolonged cultivation; and those who have the ability to give but little reason to do so now.

Then, ask yourself this question: Using which activities and which approach, how can we establish a meaningful relationship with these prospects, such that they'll want to support our work?

How long it takes to cultivate varies with each prospect. But at the very least, plan on six to eighteen months before the actual solicitation takes place.

23

WHAT YOU DON'T KNOW WILL HURT YOU

◆

Inexperienced board members often believe fund raising is merely a matter of identifying a wealthy person and persuading him or her to give.

With this approach you might if you're lucky get a token contribution, but rarely, as mentioned before, will a sizable gift come from someone you don't know.

This is why you have to learn a good deal about the people you plan to solicit.

Those in the fund raising field know that "prospect research" usually spells the difference between success and failure in raising money.

The first step is to identify individuals who, common sense says, are your most promising prospects. These of course include your current donors, but you'll also want to look at: users of your services; people who have shown an interest in your work; vendors; past and present board members; people with historical or family ties to the organization; employees; neighbors; and people interested in similar causes.

The information you'll need on these individuals includes the following: Which of them have the financial wherewithal to give; what are the prospect's giving habits; what relationship does the person have to your organization; which aspect of your cause would most interest the person; what kind of cultivation is necessary; how much will you ask for; who has the respect of the prospect; and, who is the right person to do the asking?

Yes, it can be a slow process, and, yes, the temptation is to just go out and ask. But unless you learn about your prospect and his or her interests, you can't know what the prospect is capable of giving nor the approach that is likely to work best.

24

WHO LEADS INFLUENCES WHO GIVES

◆

While the development staff does much of the legwork, as well as the planning and training, fund raising ultimately succeeds because of the time and effort community leaders put in.

For this reason the most important act, once you've decided to conduct a campaign, is to identify and recruit an effective chairperson. The right person will almost certainly influence the amount you raise.

The profile of the ideal person might look like this: He or she is wealthy, influential, generous to a range of causes, and is recognized in the community as a real leader.

Since such pillars aren't readily available,

consider yourself lucky if you land a candidate with the first two attributes - affluence and influence.

Once you've identified a promising candidate, ask yourself the following questions:

❑ Is this person experienced in organizing people, in working with committees?

❑ Is he or she a leader, someone who easily elicits loyalty?

❑ Will this person add credibility to your campaign and motivate others to participate?

❑ Will the person contribute financially and at what level?

❑ Will he or she solicit others?

❑ Does your candidate have the time and energy required?

❑ And, finally, is the person an appropriate spokesperson for your cause?

To have a real chance of succeeding, you must tap just the right person to lead your campaign. If you fail here, if you settle for second or third best, you run the very real risk of undermining your effort before it even begins.

One final note: because the general chair plays such a pivotal role, it is to your advantage to groom this person years in advance. The best candidates are campaign-seasoned board members and major donors who, by their financial commitment, have already shown they have the wealth and interest in your work.

25

TIME COMMANDS

—— ◆ ——

By nature most of us procrastinate; and when it comes to fund raising, this all-too-human tendency is a major hindrance.

It's easy to put off what you have plenty of time to do; and the more time workers have to complete their assignments, the longer they take to get started. This is one reason why a campaign timetable is essential.

Another equally important reason has to do with sequencing. To succeed in fund raising, you must solicit your best prospects first, those who can give large gifts and hopefully set the pace for others.

A timetable — one reflecting the fact that big gifts take longer to secure than small ones — will help you concentrate on these top people and prevent you from prematurely jumping to lower-level givers just because your campaign seems at a standstill.

Still other important reasons for a well-conceived timetable: it provides benchmarks to measure your progress and it gives your campaign momentum and a sense of urgency.

Start with the projected date for the end of each campaign phase and work backward. And whether you organize your timetable by week or month, include in it planning meetings, training sessions, kickoff, report meetings, and special events.

As important as scheduling is, however, don't be rigid. Fund raising is a part-time endeavor for volunteers and inevitably delays will occur. Therefore, be realistic -- make your timetable long enough to accomplish tasks, but short enough to hold the volunteers' interest.

One final note: To help ensure your target dates are met, schedule meetings as deadlines against which to press for action. A board member or volunteer, knowing campaign leaders will be attending, will do his or her best to complete assignments before the meeting.

26

STAY ON TOP
OR GO UNDER

———◆———

While campaign newsletters, phone calls, and report meetings help keep a campaign worker focused, what really spurs him or her to get the job done is personal follow-up by campaign leaders. The rule for success is always, Whoever recruits the worker is personally responsible for that person completing the task.

The campaign chairperson is responsible for recruiting and motivating the people he or she enlists, and they in turn are responsible for recruiting and motivating the workers on their teams. This helps to divide the work and ensure that everyone has someone to answer to.

While the principal reason campaigns fail is because not enough people go out and actually ask for money, campaigns also falter when indifference sets in. Perhaps a good part of the goal is in and people are feeling confident; perhaps summer vacations loom; perhaps the excitement of the campaign is simply wearing off — whatever the reason momentum is stalled.

To combat everyone's natural tendency to slow down, there are a number of strategies to use:

❑ Structure your campaign so that all chairs must keep in regular touch with their leaders, and those leaders in touch with their workers.

❑ Establish deadlines and prod each person to complete assignments on schedule.

❑ Pay special attention to unfinished solicitations, especially those involving your top prospects.

❑ Use a troubleshooting committee to focus on key problems.

❑ Hold a rally, midway through your campaign, at which all chairs and leaders report their progress.

There's no doubt fund raising is rigorous; even your best leaders will be subject to slumps. But by continually stressing personal accountability, you will shorten these slow-downs considerably.

27

TRAINING BEGETS BIGGER GIFTS

———◆———

Every fund drive using volunteers must include solicitor training sessions. This is true for annual appeals, and it's essential for capital drives.

No matter how virtuous and well organized a campaign, most major gift prospects still must be sold on how much to contribute. And to do this selling effectively, your organization must develop a team of highly trained solicitors.

While staff can plan the trainings, campaign leadership — including the president, trustees, campaign chair, and key committee chairs — must be involved in the sessions themselves. The presence of these leaders, whom campaign workers respect, will be duly noted.

Your training sessions should cover the three general stages in the solicitation process: preparing for the meeting; the meeting itself; and follow up. Almost always you'll emphasize the following points:

❑ Know your case, that is, the reason you're raising money.

❑ Make your own generous gift first.

❑ Be positive; there's no reason to apologize.

❑ Visit your prospects in person.

❑ Ask the prospect to consider the amount you suggest.

❑ Have a second or third meeting, if it's a large gift you seek.

❑ Get the job done — don't delay.

Now, is training still necessary if you already have a corps of knowledgeable workers? Absolutely. The majority of these people have little or no experience in soliciting gifts. While they may be poetic when describing your project, these same individuals often stumble when it comes to asking for money.

And what if you have people who *have* been involved in other fund raising drives? Is training here a waste of time? Not at all. You may have workers who have solicited in the past, but don't assume they did so with skill. Quite often the contrary is true. The gift they secured could have been much larger if they had been properly instructed.

28

THE SECRET LIES IN ASKING

———◆———

Donors give for a wide variety of reasons: fear, shame, guilt, loyalty, nostalgia, and immortality, to name but a few. But the most important reason people give is because somebody asked them.

Asking is the essence of fund raising. It's the most powerful tool you have. People rarely give generously without being asked *directly*. This goes for trustees, other inner circle groups, and prospects as well.

Now, this doesn't mean your cause is incidental. It isn't. And you must still sell your prospect on contributing. But what the person may know about your work isn't as persuasive as the fact that you are standing right in front of him or her and appealing for support.

Nearly every campaign would succeed if people

weren't so afraid of asking. But the reality is that many of us are willing to do *everything* but ask.

Why? We may not fully believe in the organization. We may be afraid we'll be turned down. We're not confident about our own persuasive powers. We worry we'll be perceived as mercenary. We think asking is demeaning.

These concerns affect everyone; we're universally afraid, which is the bad news. The good news is that the fear can be lessened, though not eliminated, if the solicitor:

❑ Is well-prepared.

❑ Is genuinely enthusiastic about the cause.

❑ Possesses a degree of leverage with the prospect.

❑ Communicates a sense of urgency about the campaign. And,

❑ Is a generous giver himself or herself.

Regardless of the anxiety, solicitors must press on. There's no guarantee that if you ask you will receive; but if you don't ask, you can be assured you won't receive.

Remember too that by asking, you're giving your colleague, neighbor, or friend, the opportunity to take part in something greater than themselves. In all likelihood, they'll think more of you for your effort, not less.

29

THOSE WHO ASK MUST GIVE FIRST

———◆———

Imagine a friend drops by, all excited about a hot IPO. "This is the surest thing since Ma Bell," he asserts. "You gotta buy it."

As you're about to dial your broker, you offhandedly ask how many shares your pal has bought. "None yet, but I think you should load up!" Thanks, you say as you put down the receiver, but I'll wait and see what you do.

In a similar way, before you can hope to persuade another person to support your cause, you must demonstrate your own belief by contributing. There's nothing like a generous gift to show you mean business. Not only will this make you a more enthusiastic advocate, it gives you added leverage during your visit.

It's quite effective when you can say, "John,

I've contributed $10,000 to this project. I believe it's so important I'm asking you to do the same." Think of the credibility gap if you were asked about your own level of support and you hadn't given.

Your prospects are interested in knowing what you, as a representative of the cause, have contributed. Tell them, which won't be embarrassing if you've given in proportion to your means.

Further, make your pledge early in the campaign. Not only will this deepen your commitment but, since peer solicitation is so important in fund raising, your gift will indicate the level of prospect to which you should be assigned.

"But I give my time," some will insist, "and time *is* money." Tell your grocer you'll volunteer an hour to pay for a bagful of leeks and see what he says.

Time is not the same as money. You cannot pay your staff or buy your office supplies with your time. *Both* are equally important commitments for a board member.

30

NOT ALL DONORS ARE EQUAL

◆

Even before your campaign is announced, you must identify your big-gift prospects. This allows you to concentrate on this smaller group, develop special cultivation activities, and see that proper workers make the call.

Rating your potential donors is especially important in light of the fact — borne out over and over — that the lion's share of your support will come from the top 10 percent of your prospects. These are the people who will make or break your campaign.

Too, rating allows you to arrive at a dollar figure to suggest to your top prospects.

The group doing the rating — and these must be people of equal standing to your prospects — looks primarily for three pieces of information:

the right amount to suggest to the prospect, his or her areas of interest, and who the best solicitor will be.

Among the matters to consider are: How wealthy is the prospect? Is he or she close to your organization? Does the person give to other charitable causes and how much? On that prospect's priority list how high would your organization be? And, finally, do any of your committee members have influence over the prospect?

Raters shouldn't be concerned with what prospects *might* give, or even whether they *will* give. What you want to learn from the session is what a person, if motivated properly, *could* give in light of his or her personal circumstances.

In other words, you want to know the financial capacity of the person regardless of any negative feelings toward your organization (which you would hope to change through cultivation activities).

You can bet some board members will balk at prospect rating, but it is vital. It turns up information that's helpful to your solicitors; it demonstrates to potential donors that your campaign is thought out; and it gives those whom you solicit a context for deciding what to give.

31

EACH
ACCORDING
TO HIS MEANS

◆

A common fallacy in fund raising is that a campaign can succeed if every prospect gives the same amount.

In other words, to raise $100,000 dollars, all you need to do is ask 100 people to give $1,000.

But for a number of reasons this "identical amount" approach doesn't work.

Firstly, it ignores reality. Not everyone who is asked will give. In fact you'll usually need to approach three or four prospects to secure one gift.

Secondly, not everyone will contribute, say, $1,000, which means to achieve an average gift of $1,000, gifts far greater than $1,000 will be needed.

Thirdly, asking for $1,000 in effect limits those who could or would give more.

Now if these aren't reasons enough, here's another. The "identical amount" approach isn't even fair.

We don't live in a society where wealth is distributed equally. How equitable is it, then, to ask a tycoon for the same amount as a middle-manager with four kids? Not very, and yet that's what this approach espouses.

The key to successful fund raising is seeking *proportionate* gifts; each prospect is asked to contribute an amount that, based upon his or her means, is considered generous.

Recognize the "identical amount" approach for the fallacy it is. Instead, research your prospects, carefully rate them in terms of their capacity to give, then seek a generous and proportionate gift.

Keep in mind what Irving Warner, a veteran fund raiser, said years ago:

"The man who suggests you need 1,000 contributions of $10 each for your $10,000 project:

A) Knows arithmetic

B) Thinks he's given you a brilliant solution.

C) Won't give more than $10."

32

BIG BEFORE LITTLE

In any serious fund raising campaign, the first people you solicit should be those who have the greatest potential to give and who are already close to your organization.

Put another way, you want to proceed from the "top down and inside out."

If gifts from your *top* prospects come in at the level you need, they'll set the standard and other gifts will relate to them. If on the other hand your lead gift is low, other gifts will drop accordingly and jeopardize your campaign.

As for soliciting from the *inside out*, this simply means you begin with inner-family prospects: your governing board first, then major gift prospects, followed by all other appropriate people.

Sequential fund raising, as this approach is known, is essential for two reasons: firstly, a relatively small number of donors will account for most of the funds you raise and the "top down, inside out" approach forces you to identify, cultivate, and solicit those who will make or break your campaign.

Secondly, you want to raise the sights of those who might give smaller amounts by showing them what other people — often their colleagues and peers — have committed. These leadership gifts set the standard, in other words.

Be aware that sequential fund raising does demand discipline, however.

A big gift almost always takes longer to secure than a smaller one. As a result, there's a lot more activity in soliciting lower-level donors. Some board members, impatient with the measured pace of major givers, may want to advance to the lower level. But as you will lose the leverage that sequential fund raising provides, this is a mistake.

Remember, 90 percent of your gifts will come from about 10 percent of your donors. So, despite the sometimes slow pace, spend 90 percent of your time on this pivotal 10 percent.

33

TEAMS WORK

◆

When approaching your top prospects, it's almost always advantageous to use solicitation teams. Not only do team members boost each other's courage, they're usually better able to answer the many questions that arise during the visit.

Generally speaking, the following teams (listed in order of effectiveness) work best: volunteer and organization's CEO; volunteer and staff member; CEO and staff member. But if you feel more people are needed, simply determine who they should be and bring them. For your best prospects, you'll almost always want to include your CEO.

Needless to say, not every organization has the personnel to use the team approach, especially when there are hundreds of prospects. As for solo soliciting, the order of effectiveness is normally the CEO, then the development officer, and finally the volunteer (who will usually have a hard time making the presentation alone unless he or she is intimately familiar with your work).

In addition to increasing the effectiveness of your solicitations, the team approach will serve your organization in other ways as well. Firstly, new volunteers will grow more comfortable with the asking process (which can have spill-over benefits for your annual giving program, special events, and future campaigns).

Secondly, more than one of your organization's volunteers will come to know important prospects, which will prove helpful if the person you've relied upon isn't available in the future.

Finally, your volunteers will usually have more fun, and be even more enthusiastic about your cause when they share in the asking process.

34

OVERLOADED SOLICITORS UNDERPRODUCE

◆

One sure way to get token contributions is to overload your solicitors with prospects.

Experience over the years shows that it's reasonable to expect an individual solicitor to make five personal calls. If a worker has more, he or she will probably procrastinate, or perhaps worse, use the telephone or mail to contact the prospect. Even if the worker does make the visits, there's a real possibility they will be perfunctory.

Factor in not only the personal visit, but the usual follow-up calls and letters, and it is clear that even a limited number of solicitations can be time-consuming.

When assigning prospects, you'll find some

solicitors prefer to choose the names of people they know. Others, not wanting to confront their friends, prefer people they don't know. Still others select new names in an effort to expand their contacts in the community.

These preferences can usually be granted, so long as they don't conflict with your need to make the best match.

When assigning prospects keep in mind the following suggestions:

❑ Assign your best prospects to your most influential askers.

❑ Try to get two or more committee members to work as teams on top people.

❑ Try to give everyone at least one assignment that will result in a contribution.

❑ Make sure every committee member has made a generous gift in advance.

Expect some enthusiastic workers to ask for more than five assignments. But rather than hand these out, let the worker know there'll be plenty more once they've completed the initial five.

By the same token, accept that some workers will be able to handle only one or two calls well.

35

A MATCH
MUST BE MADE

◆

Who is the best person to solicit a prospective donor?

Some insist it's a peer of the prospect, others say the CEO's organizational grasp makes him or her the most effective, while still others lobby for the development staff.

Unfortunately, there's no one right answer for all solicitations. What can be said with certainty, however, is this: each prospect should be asked by that person, or team of persons, with the best chance of securing the gift.

In order to identify the best solicitor, you must:

A) Know as much as you can about your prospect.

B) Think through what approach is likely to

work best. And,

C) Recognize that whether the solicitor is the CEO, a volunteer, or a friend, the prospect must have a good degree of *respect* for the person.

Is the considerable effort involved in matching the asker and prospect worth it? Does it matter that much? Absolutely. The size of the gift usually reflects the effectiveness of the asker.

Because inadequate attention is often paid to matching, many campaigns fall short of their goal. What happens is, the wrong solicitor ventures out and merely takes the order rather than influences the prospect. The result is a gift that could have been many times greater with the right solicitor.

36

BEING THERE IS KEY

◆

If you want major gifts, you have to ask for them in person. Very few donors will give substantially unless you stand before them and make a request.

Why? Because giving money away is hard for almost everyone. To overcome our reluctance, we not only need to be asked by someone we respect, we practically require the pressure of a face-to-face meeting.

When a solicitor calls upon a prospect, it is a powerful statement. It says in effect: I'm dedicated to this cause and believe it's important enough that I've personally come to see you.

Anxiety arises, to be sure. For no matter how much experience you have, or what training you've undergone, you'll still be nervous when calling upon a prospective donor. You can, however, mitigate your fears if you follow an "agenda" such as the following:

❑ Prepare for your meeting by studying the information you have on the prospect.

❑ Begin by thanking him or her for taking the time to meet with you.

❑ Engage in small talk to get comfortable.

❑ Talk about your organization and its mission and succinctly explain the project for which you're raising money.

❑ Discuss your own interest and involvement.

❑ If asked, let the prospect know the amount you've contributed.

❑ Invite questions.

❑ Ask for the gift. And,

❑ Express thanks if the donor gives and leave (if he or she isn't ready to give, set a time when you can return to take the matter up again).

It's also important to understand what *not* to do during a solicitation: don't browbeat, don't con, don't overstate the need, don't promise what you can't deliver. And, don't think any prospect is going to be easy to persuade.

It's tempting to make excuses why you can't go out and ask in person. But the fact remains, if you want thoughtful and proportionate gifts, you must go see your prospect. He or she deserves nothing less.

37

MORE ALIKE
THAN NOT

◆

You will usually be effective in securing contributions if you remember one thing: to think like your prospects.

They may have more money and more power than you, but they still share many of the same concerns, problems, worries, and anxieties.

Like you, they're interested in helping. Like you, they're busy and want you to be direct. Like you, they respond favorably to dedicated people. And like you, they will give.

Too often organizations keep prospects at a distance, as if this were the preferred means of cultivation. Hardly. It makes much more sense to treat these individuals — who are in fact your best hope for the future — as friends, not pariahs.

At all times strive to see each prospect as a

person, not an assignment. Better yet, see them as yourself, for at this very moment you are probably somebody's prospect yourself.

How would you want to be treated? Like a normal person, with respect and sensitivity. After all, you and your prospect are partners working toward a shared goal.

Approached in the right way, fund raising isn't a hard sell and shouldn't be viewed as such. It is simply an appeal to the heart and a noble attempt to advance humanity.

38

NO APOLOGY
NEEDED

◆

When you approach someone for a gift, there's no need to feel ashamed or embarrassed. You aren't begging; you're appealing on behalf of a worthy cause from which you gain nothing financially.

Don't demean your effort or your cause by saying how sorry you are to ask.

An apology is inappropriate, especially when you consider that those who give large gifts usually accept the responsibility for sharing their resources. For many, it's a way of expressing gratitude for their good fortune. They gain a sense of self-worth from their philanthropy.

You're a solicitor, not a supplicant, and your job is to help the person understand your organization's mission, one in which you believe and have contributed to as well.

Then, as John D. Rockefeller, one of the most solicited men in history, said many years ago, the "duty of giving is as much his as is the duty of asking yours."

In fact, Rockefeller's gracious outlook on solicitors, is worth recounting here:

"When a solicitor comes to you and lays on your heart the responsibility that rests so heavily on his; when his earnestness gives convincing evidence of how seriously interested he is; when he makes it clear that he knows you are no less anxious to do your duty in the matter than he is, that you are just as conscientious, that he feels sure all you need is to realize the importance of the enterprise and the urgency of the need in order to lead you to do your full share in meeting it — he has made you his friend and has brought you to think of giving not as a duty but as a privilege."

39

MISSION, ABOVE ALL

———◆———

The mission of your organization, rather than a particular project, is what ultimately determines whether your best prospects will give.

These people must believe in the organization itself and identify with its mission and goals. The programs or projects carried out to fulfill the mission are important, but less so.

As Henry Rosso, founder of The Fund Raising School, puts it, your overarching mission is the magnet that attracts and holds the interest of major donors. It is more important than any single project or program, more important in fact than the history of your organization, the solicitor, your distinct offerings, or your project's aims.

Before beginning any solicitations, you must be prepared to respond to a host of questions about your mission. Among these are:

❑ Why do you exist in the first place?

❑ What is distinctive about you?

❑ Why do you feel you merit support?

❑ What is it that you want to accomplish and how do you intend to do it?

❑ How will you hold yourself accountable?

You can be sure your prospects will voice these questions, outwardly or inwardly. And if satisfactory answers aren't forthcoming, they will withhold support.

Unless your potential donor is already *intimately* familiar with your organization, focus on your mission first. Sell it before you sell your project. You won't attract a meaningful gift unless you do.

40

GET PERSONAL

—◆—

How can you make your project personal for your prospective donor? This is a question you must always ask before making your solicitation call.

People won't support you simply because you want them to. But they will give when they see a personal benefit or when you translate your campaign into compelling human terms.

Take Alzheimers research. For scientists in the lab, it is all about test tubes, microbes, and chemical compounds. But for your prospects it's something else altogether. It is hope they and their family will be spared this debilitating disease.

Or, say you're raising money to upgrade your local library. It is far more effective to stress, not the need for computers or shelf space, but the importance of the facility as an exploring ground for young minds, where curiosity is nurtured.

You can make this same sort of "human case" for colleges, museums, hospitals, for virtually any organization.

But to do so you must know your "product." That is, you must be familiar with the aims of your organization, who it serves, how it affects people's lives, *and* you must have a real sense of your prospects' needs, wants, hopes, and ambitions.

Attempt to identify one or two possible projects that match what you believe are your prospect's interests. Then, after gaining support for your organization's overall mission, present these projects, document their need, and show the benefits that will result if either or both are funded.

Be sure the projects are challenging, however. Major donors usually want to do something special, something others may not be able to do. As a result, they tend toward those projects having the potential to create a lasting change for the good.

41

GO FIGURE

◆

Say you're approached by a fellow office worker and asked to pitch in for a colleague's wedding gift. The first question you'll typically ask is, "How much do you have in mind?" or "What are others giving?"

What you're seeking is a frame of reference.

The same dynamic is at work when you approach prospects — you must tell them what you *hope* they'll contribute or what their peers are giving.

This need to ask for a *specific* gift unsettles some volunteers. While many are willing to ask for "any amount you can manage," or "as much as you can afford," the thought of citing a figure creates anxiety. Many volunteers worry they'll embarrass or anger the prospect.

But rarely will the person get upset, especially if your request is phrased properly: "We're hoping you'll consider a gift in the range of $50,000," or, "Will you consider joining me in giving $25,000 to this worthy cause?"

To the contrary, the prospect is usually grateful for the parameters (and sees too that you've given your campaign careful thought). While he or she may not be able to give the amount you suggest, the individual will often stretch to give more than originally intended.

Another, perhaps "softer" way to frame the request is to mention what others are doing, without naming names of course. Or, you can stress that your organization needs several friends to contribute at a certain level and you're hoping the prospect will consider being among them.

To fail to ask for a specific gift is to invite a far smaller gift than you might otherwise secure. You cannot insist on a figure -- it is after all a suggestion only. But voiced properly it is one that forces the prospect to ponder the seriousness of your request and to respond.

42

ASK OR
ALL IS LOST

◆

Almost all effective solicitations contain four stages:

1) The introduction, during which pleasantries are exchanged.

2) A discussion allowing the prospect to express personal views about the organization.

3) An explanation of the need and the benefits for the prospect.

4) A closing during which time a gift is requested.

This last stage, the most vital, is also the most threatening, which explains why it's often bypassed.

Many a solicitor has spoken eloquently about the cause, has persuasively made the case for supporting the project, has had the prospect all but ready to commit, only to drop the ball by failing to close the sale.

Asking is the most difficult part of the meeting; it is when the heart starts pounding. But unless you ask, everyone's time is wasted; the prospect's, the solicitor's, and the staff whose support work has all been directed toward this moment.

From the time you walk in the door, keep your eyes on your goal — securing a specific gift from the prospect. Let this guide every aspect of your conversation.

You can phrase your request in any number of ways:

❑ Would you join with me in making a gift of....

❑ Would you become a part of this effort by making a gift of...

❑ We hope you will consider a gift of...

But make sure you ask, and once you've asked say nothing more. You'll want to break the silence; you'll want to relieve the tension; you'll want to jump in and say a smaller gift would be all right, too. But don't.

No matter how long it takes, let your prospect be the next to speak. It takes courage, but as any pro will tell you, it is one of the secrets to success when raising serious money.

43

RETURN VISITS REQUIRED

———◆———

It comes as a surprise to many volunteers, but securing a major gift often requires two or three visits with the prospect.

It depends largely on the person's readiness to give, how much he or she knows about your organization, how effective your cultivation has been, and how accurately you've pinpointed the prospect's particular interests.

In many cases, you'll use your first and second meetings for fact-finding and cultivation, not for soliciting.

During these visits you'll acquaint the prospect with your objectives and the need for substantial pledges. You'll also assess how he or she feels about your organization. And, you'll learn about the prospect's specific interests.

What you gain from these initial meetings will prepare you for your most important meeting, when you do in fact ask.

Don't expect to walk away from your first visit with a check in hand. If you do receive a gift, chances are it is much smaller than it could have been had you taken the time to nurture the relationship.

44

GRATITUDE TO ONE AND ALL

◆

The story goes that when Booker T. Washington was raising money for Tuskegee Institute, he received a letter from John D. Rockefeller containing a single dollar.

Many would have been insulted, but not Washington. He wrote Rockefeller a gracious thank-you and at the end of the fiscal year, sent the oil baron an exact accounting of what he'd done with the dollar.

It won't surprise you that Rockefeller began his real support of Tuskegee shortly thereafter.

As this perhaps apocryphal story illustrates, thanking donors is more than good manners, it's the first step in cultivating the next gift.

All contributions, even those of a few dollars, should be acknowledged if only with a *prompt* official receipt. First-time donors merit a brief letter from the CEO welcoming them to the organizational family.

Of course, for major donors you'll want to pull out the stops. A personal letter, including an invitation to a luncheon, may be appropriate. Complimentary tickets to a special event would be another possibility. For the very highest level donor, you may wish to arrange a small dinner party as your way of showing appreciation.

If you think you don't have time for thanking, keep the following in mind: prior donors are your best prospects for future gifts; at least half will send you a second gift of the same amount; and, after making a third gift, a donor is likely to continue giving for five or more years.

In reality, you can never thank your donors enough.

45

THE FINAL STEP
IS THE ASKING

———◆———

It has been said that fund raising is 90 percent preparation and 10 percent asking. To those who think soliciting alone *is* fund raising, this often comes as a great surprise.

Fund raising isn't simply a matter of identifying wealthy people and asking them to give. Only those who are naive think this. No, raising serious money is a comprehensive process.

Before the actual solicitation come a host of steps: planning, recruiting the right leaders, preparing your arguments, researching and rating your prospects, cultivating these people, and matching the right solicitor to the prospect.

Only when each of these steps has been accomplished, are you truly prepared for the actual solicitation, which should then be relatively easy.

At that point, you will have meaningfully involved the prospect in your organization, shared your vision and goals, and documented their importance to the community if not to humankind.

In all likelihood, the person will then choose to make an investment in your organization, one as big as his swelling heart.

46

SIMPLICITY PREVAILS

—— ◆ ——

When all is said and done, there are no real mysteries to successful fund raising. Instead there are tested techniques. These allow you to raise the most money in the shortest period of time at the least expense.

Each of the important ones has been discussed in this book, from the need to recruit top leadership to prospect research to gift tables to asking for a specific amount.

Detailing the process, as I've done here, can make fund raising seem complicated. But it isn't really, especially if you remember a few simple rules:

❑ Learn as much about your organization as you can.

❑ Make your own gift first, and make it

proportionate to your means.

❑ Know your prospect.

❑ Visit him or her in person.

❑ Let your prospect know how much you have given and ask for the amount you hope he'll give.

❑ Be quiet and let your prospect respond.

And keep one other thing in mind too.

Fund raising has been a part of the American landscape since the birth of our nation. Thousands of colleges, hospitals, museums, and human service programs have come into being because individuals have cared enough to go out and ask.

If you find your enthusiasm ebbing, remember, as a participant you are in the fine company of sincere, dedicated, and optimistic people willing to work tirelessly for a better world.

Not many of us can say the same.

47

AN EVALUATION ENLIGHTENS

◆

To understand why you succeeded or failed, you must at the end of your campaign evaluate your results and make recommendations for the future.

What was good about your campaign and what was pointless? To answer this, you will need to examine the following:

Expenses

Where was money put to good use, where was it wasted?

Materials

Which campaign materials were useful, which were seldom used?

Meetings

Were there too many, too few, and what kind were the most productive?

Solicitations

Which worked best, team solicitations or solo visits, volunteers or staff?

Future leaders

Which workers distinguished themselves and should be tapped for other posts in your organization?

If, in fact, your campaign failed, or didn't achieve what you hoped, you will want to look at the following as well:

Timing

Was your campaign poorly timed? For example, was a more popular organization soliciting your prospects ahead of you?

Commitment

Did your leadership grasp the importance of the campaign and accept its urgency?

Potential donors

Did you have enough legitimate prospects, those with some link to your organization, with the ability to give, and with interest in your cause?

Inner-family giving

Did your board of directors give generously and proportionately?

Realistic goal

Was your goal realistic, that is, was it based upon the pledges of your inner-family and the careful rating of your prospects? Was it in line with what your consultant suggested?

Publicity

Did you rely on publicity, rather than personal visits, to raise money?

Leadership

Did you have strong leadership that made a plan, stuck to deadlines, and followed up on loose ends?

Candid answers to these questions will reveal why your campaign foundered. Put all of this information in writing. And do it while the campaign is still fresh in your mind.

Companion Book
to Fund Raising Realities

ASKING

A 59-Minute Guide to Everything
Board Members, Volunteers, and Staff
Must Know to Secure the Gift

by Jerold Panas, 112 pp. $24.95

It ranks right up there with public speaking. Nearly all of us fear it. And yet it's critical to our success. *Asking for money*. It makes even the stout-hearted quiver.

But now comes a book, *Asking: A 59-Minute Guide to Everything Board Members, Staff and Volunteers Must Know to Secure the Gift*. And short of a medical elixir, it's the next best thing for emboldening you, your board members and volunteers to ask with skill, finesse ... and powerful results.

Jerold Panas, who as a staff person, board member and volunteer has secured gifts ranging from $50 to $50 million, understands the art of asking perhaps better than anyone in America.

He has harnessed all of his knowledge and experience and produced a landmark book.

What *Asking* convincingly shows — and one reason staff will applaud the book and board members will devour it — is that it doesn't take stellar communication skills to be an effective asker. Nearly everyone, regardless of their persuasive ability, can become an effective fundraiser if they follow Jerold Panas' step-by-step and easy to implement guidelines.

Emerson & Church, Publishers
Tel. 508-359-0019 • Fax 508-359-2703

Additional Titles in the Series,
The Gold Standard of Board Books

The Ultimate Board Member's Book

A 1-Hour Guide to Understanding and Fulfilling
Your Role & Responsibilities • Kay Sprinkel Grace • $24.95

Here is a book for *all* board members: those needing an
orientation to the unique responsibilities of a nonprofit board;
those wishing to clarify exactly what their individual role is; and
those hoping to fulfill their charge with maximum effectiveness.

It's all here in 120 tightly organized and jargon-free pages:
how boards work, what the job entails, the time commitment,
the role of staff, serving on committees and task forces, fundraising
responsibilities, conflicts of interest, group decision-making,
effective recruiting, de-enlisting board members, board self-
evaluation, and more.

Fundraising Mistakes that Bedevil All Boards

A 1-Hour Guide to Identifying and Overcoming Obstacles
to Your Success • Kay Sprinkel Grace • $24.95

Fundraising mistakes are a thing of the past. If you err from
now on, it simply shows you haven't read this acclaimed book.
A sampling of the *40* mistakes that Grace *refutes*:
- "People will give just because yours is a good cause."
- "Wealth is what determines a person's willingness to give."
- "You need a powerful board to have a successful campaign."
- "Tax deductibility is a powerful incentive."
- "Estate gifts only come from big donors."

How Are We Doing?

A 1-Hour Guide to Evaluating Your Performance
as a Nonprofit Board • Gayle L. Gifford • $24.95

Until now, almost all books on board evaluation have had an
air of unreality about them. The perplexing graphs, the matrix
boxes, the overlong questionnaires.

Enter Gayle Gifford, a renowned trainer who has pioneered
an elegantly simple way for boards to improve their overall
performance. It all comes down to answering a host of straight-
forward questions.

It doesn't matter whether the setting is formal or casual,
whether you have 75 board members or seven, or whether yours
is an established institution or a grassroots start-up. All that
matters is that you answer the questions candidly.

For quantity discounts, call 508-359-0019

Copies of this and other books from
the publisher are available at discount
when purchased in quantity for
boards of directors or staff.

Emerson
& Church
PUBLISHERS

P.O. Box 338 • Medfield, MA 02052
Tel. 508-359-0019 • Fax 508-359-2703
www.emersonandchurch.com